THE ART OF REVISION

Writing is Rewriting

**WRITING LESSONS FROM THE FRONT
BOOK 12**

ANGELA HUNT

Hunt Haven Press

The Art of Revision, Copyright 2023, Angela Hunt.
Published by Hunt Haven Press. All rights reserved. Do not reproduce or share these pages without permission from the publisher.

ISBN: 978-1961394179

OTHER LESSONS IN THE SERIES

1. *The Plot Skeleton*
2. *Creating Extraordinary Characters*
3. *Point of View*
4. *Track Down the Weasel Words*
5. *Evoking Emotion*
6. *Plans and Processes to Get Your Book Written*
7. *Tension on the Line*
8. *Writing Historical Fiction*
9. *The Fiction Writer's Book of Checklists*
10. *Writing the Picture Book*
11. *The First Fifty Pages of your Novel*
12. *The Art of Revision*
A Christian Writer's Possibly Useful Ruminations on a Life in Pages, supplemental volume

The first ten books are available in one volume, Writing Lessons from the Front, the first ten books.
Paperback ISBN: 978-0692311134
Hardcover ISBN: 978-1961394100

Visit Angela Hunt's website at www.angelahuntbooks.com.

INTRODUCTION

Revision: a time to reread, revisit, reconsider, re-examine, refocus, realign, reform, and reimagine that which has gone before. The saving grace of being able to go back, as many times as necessary, to make certain your first effort is not your final effort, and your work is the best it can be.

Welcome to the art of revision. This lesson is similar to *The Fiction Writer's Book of Checklists*, but I wanted to revisit the subject, to go a little deeper and speak to people who don't necessarily respond to checklists.

I often answer writing questions on Quora.com, and I've noticed that many new writers are confused about revision. They may show their first or second draft to friends and receive confusing or contradictory reports. How should they proceed? How do they know that tinkering with the story won't make the book worse?

This lesson will give you a simple and straightforward way to revise your first draft—think of it as analogous to taking your car into the mechanic's shop. He'll tune up your engine by methodically checking every element of the car—the carburetor, the ignition system, the fuel injectors, the exhaust, the brakes, and—well, I've run out of automotive terms. I'm not a mechanic.

But I am a writer, and I've developed a thorough system for revising a manuscript. This lesson will explain that system. If you follow these principles, you can be sure you are making your novel or short story the best it can be.

By the way: I'm a nuts-and-bolts kind of teacher, and I tend to firmly say, "Don't do this" and "Do this instead." I'm sure you will realize that exceptions *are* allowed—after all, writing is an art, not a science. But nine times out of ten, you'll be better off if you follow the instructions in this lesson. I've been writing a long time, I've studied dozens of writing craft books, and I've learned from some amazingly talented experts. My goal in these writing lessons is to boil things down to basics and give you clear instructions. You're free to take them or leave them.

Ready? Let's go!

THE FIRST DRAFT

I laughed the other day when someone on the Quora platform asked: "Should I begin with a rough draft or write something closer to the final product?"

My answer? "By all means, make this draft as perfect as possible, because when you're finished, you're going to have a rough draft."

Every first draft needs revision. Alton Gansky, a writer friend of mine, once pointed out that if you have a 100,000-word manuscript that is 99.9 percent perfect, you're still going to have 100 mistakes.

But the art of revision isn't so much about finding typos, missing words, or misstatements—it's about asking yourself, "Is this the *best* way to write this scene? This character? This emotion?" Revision is about polishing and rewriting until you have examined, enhanced, and elevated every word, phrase, paragraph, and chapter to its highest level. And here's the clincher—the more you learn about writing, the more you want to revise. The more you yearn to produce an unforgettable and life-changing work.

But don't think your book has to be filled with multisyllabic words and read like a literary tome. Novels are about providing emotion, entertainment, and escape, not showing off your vocabulary. Writing, like most jobs, isn't about *you*, it's about your customer. You write for a reader, so you must reach that reader on his or her level. The most successful novelists realize that theirs is an others-oriented profession, and they write to be *invisible*. They want the reader to get caught up in the story, not in the writer's ability to sling words around.

If you already have a first draft, great. But if you don't, let me urge you to start writing with one principle in mind—first drafts are for *getting the story down*. For putting the words onto paper or into the computer.

First drafts are not for displaying your brilliance, perfect prose, or zippy quotes. If you have deep thoughts and well-honed phrases, by all means get them down. But mostly, first drafts are for creating something out of a few random thoughts and a scrawny plot outline.

I cannot tell you how many people have told me that they've always wanted to write a novel. Some of them even begin to write. But once they get a few words onto the page, they spend hours agonizing over those words. Every day they begin at chapter one, tweaking and changing and cutting and pasting and making very little forward progress.

First drafting isn't about editing, it's about moving forward. Pull the words out of your head and send them through your fingertips into your chosen receptacle. If you absolutely *must* look at what you wrote the day before, okay, read the previous scene and then plunge ahead. If you want to change something, make a footnote or jot thoughts in the margin, but don't take more than a couple of minutes to stop and tinker.

Forward motion, remember?

Lots of people spend all their time agonizing over the books they *could* publish if they didn't spend all their time agonizing.

Revision is vitally important, but we're going to revise later, I promise. In the first draft, we're going to focus on getting that baby birthed. So don't stop.

But what if you don't have all the information you need? Can you stop and look it up?

You can wait. Insert a bracket and keep going.

Let's say I have Donnie and Susie going to visit her father's grave in Lincoln, Nebraska. I've set my novel in a real town, so I want to use an actual graveyard. In my first draft, I would write:

> Donnie parked at the concrete curb and stared out the window. [find it] Cemetery, the sign said. An aging oak sheltered the granite tombstones with protective limbs.

Don't break your momentum to do an internet search for the name of a cemetery in Nebraska. You'll have time for that later.

Between drafts, I usually schedule a couple of days for "triage," a concept I learned from Sol Stein. I use those days to fix the places in immediate need of repair. I search for brackets and find what I need to look up, then I locate the answers and write them in. Seek-and-find is easy work, and you don't have to be "in the writing zone" to insert those details.

Writing programs like Scrivener have a "notes" window off to the side, where you can make notes to yourself—things like "Don't forget that Uncle George is also buried here, so Susie would remark on it." In a later draft, you'll see that note and make the proper insertion.

If you write in Windows, you can use the "insert/comment" or even the "footnote" feature to create reminders for yourself.

How do you keep the momentum of a first draft going?

You might give yourself a daily word count—depending on how many hours you have to write each day, make yourself stop when you've hit your quota. Don't quit when you run out of steam; quit when you're in the middle of a writing rush. When you return to writing the next day, your unfinished paragraph, quote, or thought will help you pick up exactly where you left off.

It's also helpful to have your scenes sketched out on notecards, so you always know what's coming next. You can do this before you begin writing, but I prefer to do it in stages. I'll do all the scene cards for the first act, and when those pages are written, I'll do the scene cards for the second act. Not doing them beforehand leaves room for the new ideas and plot developments that pop into my head.

If you *do* hit a wall, get up and take a brisk walk. Or take a nap. Sometimes your subconscious will percolate while you do something else, and the idea or the words you need will be waiting when you return to your desk.

If you feel like you're writing garbage, type: "I'm writing garbage, but it's all I can think of," and keep going. I've done that more times than I can count—and sometimes the lines that seemed like garbage are actually not so bad in hindsight. And if they *are* truly terrible, by the time of the second draft my head has cleared and I'm able to write something better.

Finally, remember this—when compared to a revised draft, first drafts are always awful. I have a writing friend who has told her husband that if she dies with a first draft on her computer, her hubby is to pretend it doesn't exist. No one wants—or should want—their first draft to be published.

Don't be surprised if your first draft is short on the word

count—mine are usually only half of what the finished book will be. That's okay—you will add more depth, texture, and emotion in the revision process. Think of your book as an onion and write in layers.

Are you ready? If you don't have a first draft, start writing!

THE SECOND DRAFT

If you're ready to begin your rewrite, you should have a first draft either sitting on your desk or waiting on your computer. Congratulations! Creating a first draft is the hardest part of writing. Producing a first draft is like birthing a baby—it involves a lot of groaning, buckets of sweat, some muttering, and occasional screaming.

But now your messy, screaming darling is ready for the revision process. Your newborn may be a bona fide mess, but at least it *exists*. Do you know how many people say they're going to write a book and never do?

So congratulations! You've written a first draft, and that's saying something. If writing a book was easy, everybody would do it.

Now you have to realize that your first draft, especially if this is your first book, is *not* ready to be published. Trust me on this. Many full-time writers keep their first book in a drawer, where it lives in quiet anonymity. To them, writing that first book was a learning experience that prepared them for the work ahead.

I always roll my eyes when writer-characters in movies

type "The End" on a manuscript and break open the bubbly, as if their first draft is their final draft. That is not realistic. Professional writers know the first draft is only a rough approximation of what the book will ultimately be.

Every first draft needs revision.

Continuing with the baby analogy, what do you do with a newborn? You pick it up, count its fingers and toes, and clean it up. You wrap it in a blanket and feed it. Later, when you're no longer exhausted from the process of childbirth, you dress the child in cute clothes and show it off to friends and family. A little later, you send it to school, where other people mold your beloved child from elementary school through graduation.

The writing process is a lot like that. When your first draft is done, you should take a few days to recover from the first-drafting process. Do your triage and fill-in those brackets. After three or four more passes, when the manuscript has been polished, you can show it to some beta readers. Finally, you'll send it off to a publisher where, if it's accepted, an editor will guide your baby through the editorial process and publication.

Create the Front Matter

In this second draft, let's begin with the front matter—the pages at the beginning of the book. If you haven't already, create a title page for your story, complete with your name and address (or your agent's) in the upper left corner, the title of the book centered in the middle of the page, and your name—and don't include the word "by."

Below your name, write a one-sentence synopsis of your story. Imagine that you're in an elevator with an editor or agent, and you have only thirty seconds to explain what your story is about:

Magic and danger await Dorothy Gale, a young orphan, when a tornado picks her up in Kansas and drops her in a mysterious land called Oz.

A police chief with a deathly fear of water must overcome demanding tourists and a greedy mayor when a giant shark threatens the safety of his oceanfront town.

With a dangerous hurricane approaching, three women are trapped together in an elevator, not realizing that they have something in common: the dead man on the fortieth floor.

Why do we write this brief synopsis? Knowing exactly what your story is about might help you sell it to an editor or agent. But the chief benefit is that this exercise will help *you* focus on what your story is about as you go through the revision process. Too many writers get bogged down in subplots and rabbit trails.

After you've condensed your story to a single sentence, write a paragraph that could serve as back cover copy for your story. In this copy, remember not to give away the ending. The purpose of this paragraph isn't to synopsize the story, it's to hook a reader's curiosity and reveal the genre and style of the story. If you send this to a publisher, this copy will hook the editor's interest as well. I always put it beneath my name on the title page.

Don't worry about getting this paragraph exactly right on the first try—you should edit it through each subsequent draft. But it's important to get your thoughts down.

Here's the copy I wrote for one of my novels, *Passing Strangers*:

A train roars over the rails, carrying passengers on a trip that will change their lives. Among the many people aboard the 97 Silver Meteor are Andie Crystal, a lonely young woman hiding from her youth as a reality TV star; Matthew Scofield, a widower struggling to manage his responsibilities to his two young children; and Janette Turlington, a middle-aged mother running from a situation that has destroyed the peace in her home and marriage. These three form a makeshift family on an Amtrak tour through the Southern seaboard, a journey that just might heal their wounded hearts and restore them to the people to whom they matter most.

Why are we doing things that may seem unnecessary? They aren't superfluous—you will need these tools eventually, so you might as well work on them now. Second, writing these bits forces you to corral your thoughts and narrow the focus of your story. Too often I ask writers what their story-in-progress is about and hear, "Oh, it's about a woman who does this and then that happens and this happens and then . . ."

Sharpen your focus to an ice pick's point. Being able to describe your story in one paragraph and one sentence is important.

Once you have written a paragraph of back cover copy, create a **style shee**t for your editor. What's a style sheet? It's a quick reference guide, and on it you list all the main character names, cities, and anything you want your editor to know. If you keep misspelling a certain word and spellcheck doesn't catch it, make a note on your style sheet so your editor can look for it. If, for instance, first century Christians didn't speak of their *church* but of their *ecclesia*, make a note of it. You might also list important dates in your book, to make it easier for your editor to check your consistency and the ages of your characters.

The style sheet will not be part of the final book.

You don't have to worry about the **copyright page** unless you plan to self-publish. If you are, simply type out the name of the book, the publisher, the date of publication, and the ISBN number for that particular edition (hardcover, paperback, or ebook). Add "Copyright by [Your Name] in [Year of Publication]. You may add a notice that says "All rights reserved." That is the standard notice that you own the copyright and no one should publish your material without permission. Examine the copyright notice in books like yours and create your notice in a similar fashion.

Once the copyright page is done, you might want to give some thought to an **epigraph** for your novel— a brief quotation from poetry or prose featured on a single page in the front of the book. You don't *have* to use an epigraph, but I love them because they hint at the story's theme and tone. I daresay most readers read them and forget them, but why not use one?

To find a good epigraph, consider the theme or some other element of your story. Is your story about a journey? Sisters? Family? Money?

Pull out a good book of quotations or go online and search for quotes that echo or restate this theme. You might want to jot down several options and keep them in your notes —by the time you have polished the book, one of the quotes should seem more perfect than the others. If you can't find an apt quote, create one of your own—just make sure it's poetic and lovely and perfect for your story. I couldn't find a suitable quote for my novel *The Shadow Women*, so I wrote one myself and attributed it to a pen name, Darien Haynes.

Now that you've taken care of your front matter, read the rest of this chapter. If you like visual reminder, put some of the subheads on note cards and keep them on your desk. You're going to cover a lot in this second draft, and the cards will help you stay on track.

Revise Your Plot Structure

Now that your front matter is done, it's time to count your baby's fingers and toes—in other words, it's time to make sure the key plot elements are present.

When you start to work through this manuscript again, examine your plot skeleton and make sure your story has the right bones in the right place. Do you reveal her hidden need in the first act? Have you kept backstory *out* of the first act? Is she likable? Does she have a skill or talent? Will the reader care enough about her to spend several hours in her company?

Does your story open in the middle of some action, where this character is trying to reach a goal *not* related to the main story problem? (For a refresher on this, see *The First Fifty Pages* lesson). Is the main story problem introduced after we have begun to care about the character, about 20 percent of the way into the story?

After the inciting incident when your protagonist enters the special story world, does he or she establish a film-able goal? Something we can *see,* as opposed to character growth? Character growth should also occur, so what have you written to show that the protagonist will be a different person after the events of this story?

Are there complications to the protagonist's efforts to achieve the stated goal? After character deals with a complication, is there a swing that eases the pressure? To maintain proper pacing, you don't want your protagonist to be hammered again and again and again with no respite. You'll wear out your reader.

What is your story's bleakest moment? At what point is

there is no hope of achieving the goal? At that point, who comes along to give your protagonist a push in the right direction? What decision does the character then make? What lesson does he or she learn?

These are basic story structure questions, but they are important in any story—and they are present in every story that works. Make sure your plot skeleton has all of the main story "bones."

Since many novels sag in the second act, the middle usually filled with complications and obstacles, this little tip might help you keep the action moving forward: All plots can be boiled down to man against man, man against nature, or man against himself. One of these should dominate throughout your book. But if you're writing about a man who's trying to find his kidnapped daughter and you need a break from the constant back-and-forth between villain and hero, consider a complication of man against nature. The hero is on his way to deliver the ransom money, but an unexpected tornado picks up his car and drops him ten miles away. Or one of his multiple personalities takes over and hops a jet for Vegas. You get the idea.

In your second draft, make the necessary plot adjustments and fill in missing elements. Start at the beginning and work through the manuscript, changing, adding, or cutting words as necessary. You should have filled in most of the bracketed bits during triage, so in this second draft you are working to:

- cut unnecessary rabbit trails and descriptions
- add emotion where needed
- move backstory to the back of the story
- fill in any missing scenes that are needed to clarify, add foreshadowing, introduce characters you didn't know you needed until you were first drafting, and anything else that seems obvious to you.

Remember the acronym RUE—resist the urge to explain. In previous lessons (especially *Tension on the Line*), we learned that the writer's job is to toss out hooks, not to answer the reader's questions. You don't want to confuse the reader, but you *do* want to raise provocative questions so she keeps turning those pages.

Anything in your story that does not advance plot or deepen characterization needs to be cut. Before you groan, be aware that I know how painful cutting can be. So here's a trick to make it easier. If you're writing in Word, open a new document and name it "Cut materials for Possible Use." If you're writing in Scrivener, simply make a new card and call it by the same name.

If you find that you've rambled on and on about the beauty of the beach sunset, whittle those paragraphs down by selecting, cutting, and pasting the extraneous material in your "cut materials" file. That way you haven't wasted your time and energy, you've simply moved those words to another place. Do this as you work through the story, and I'm betting you won't even miss those bits. But if you discover that you *do* need them, you'll have them.

When I wrote my first draft of *The Note*, I realized I'd written all the plot elements, but had completely ignored my protagonist's character growth. I'd been so caught up in plotting her search for the owner of a note that washed up after an airplane crash that I didn't know her at all. Who was she? What was her secret? Why was she even in the story?

Take a Look at Your Characters

Now consider your story people—before you jump into revising, make sure each character has a reason for being in the story. If you have a huge cast of characters, can you combine two or three into one? Does each character play a different role? Do your main characters have flaws and/or weaknesses as well as virtues? Have you assigned a personality type to each character? (For a quick way to create characters using the Myers-Briggs personality profiles, see the lesson *Creating Extraordinary Characters*).

Do your characters have names that are so similar that your readers may confuse them? I usually try not to have characters whose name begin with the same first letter. There's no law against that, of course, but it's easier for readers to remember characters if their names are distinctive.

Have you given each of the main characters a quirk of some kind? A distinctive appearance, speech, and/or attitude? You don't have to fully flesh out every character in the book, but the *main* characters should be well-developed.

Check the description of your characters—it may help you to write their descriptions on a notecard and double-check them. I've read too many manuscripts where Harry has brown eyes in chapter one and blue eyes in chapter five.

If you mention anything specific about a character—age, birth year, graduation year, etc., make a note of it so you can be consistent in later scenes.

Perfect people are perfectly boring. We want to root for a protagonist, but he or she needs to have at least one weakness or flaw to make him fully human. Even Superman had to deal with Kryptonite.

On the flip side, completely evil villains can come off as caricatures, so make sure to give your villain a touch of goodness or sophistication. Hannibal Lecter is a twisted psychopath, but we can't help admiring his intelligence, his brilliant deductions, and the fact that he won't harm Clarice, the protagonist of *The Silence of the Lambs*. So let your good guys have weaknesses and flaws; let your villains love something—the dog, his children, or the American dream.

Which character or characters serve as an antagonist to your main character? Not every story has a villain, because not every story is a mystery or thriller. But every novel needs an antagonist or two, because a protagonist that does not meet with opposition achieves his goal far too easily.

Consider every cop movie you've ever seen—the main character's boss is always on his case, isn't he? The sergeant or commander or whoever is always yelling about some rule, taking away the cop's gun, or doing something to make the protagonist's goal harder to reach. They're not bad people, but at some point they will *stand in the way* of the protagonist's goal.

In my Fairlawn series, I had Jennifer, a divorced mother of two, travel to Florida with her mother to check out the funeral home she'd inherited. Joella was Jen's mother, and with all her heart she hoped Jen would sell the old house and move back to Virginia where Joella lived. So when Jennifer begins to consider keeping the house and running the funeral home, Joella does everything in her power to keep that from happening. She's not evil. She loves her daughter and grandsons. But she becomes Jennifer's antagonist . . . until she realizes Jennifer needs a new life in Florida.

An antagonist can be a mother, a sister, a boss, a jealous friend, or a neighbor. A book can have several antagonists—a boss in chapter two, a criminal in chapter three, the best friend in chapter four. But it's important that some of your characters function as antagonists to complicate your protagonist's efforts to reach that all-important goal.

Your protagonist will face other obstacles—forces of nature, the restriction of time, traffic, physical limitations, being in the wrong place at the right time—but other characters will probably be the most reliable source of tension and conflict for your story. But the reason these other people oppose or support your protagonist needs to be logical. You shouldn't set a mother against her daughter for some flimsy reason. And you shouldn't have your heroine fall in love with the hero just because he has dreamy eyes.

What do you get when you squeeze a lemon? *You get whatever's inside.* You may get lemon juice. But if the fruit is rotten, there's no telling what you'll get.

All of us wear a public face when we're with people. We relax a little when we're with friends, but our true selves appear when we're stressed. Our tempers, our prejudices, our selfishness can be unveiled when we're pressed to make a quick, desperate choice.

Are you applying enough pressure to your protagonist? Many beginning novelists treat their protagonists far too gently, never squeezing the character to the point that we see the real person beneath the facade.

In *Creating Extraordinary Characters,* I explain how to make sure you are pushing your character enough. But here's an exercise from agent Donald Maass to help you apply more pressure to your main character:

Make a note of something your protagonist would never, ever think.

Now write something your protagonist would never, ever do.

Now write something your protagonist would never, ever say.

Now . . . write a scene or scenes in which your character does, says, and thinks those three things. If your novel has a villain, do the same exercise with him or her in mind, then give him a hard squeeze.

Surely you have found yourself in a place where you've said or done something you never thought you would say or do. I know I have. Remember how you felt—were you angry? Broken? In despair? Transfer those feelings to your protagonist or antagonist and watch your story get better.

Have you made your protagonist sufficiently sympathetic?

Have you put him in a situation where he's embarrassed? Rebuffed? Humiliated? Readers bond with characters when they suffer . . . because we've all been in dark places. What have you done to make your characters' lives miserable?

Have you made your protagonist sufficiently strong and admirable? Have we seen her exhibit a particular talent? Is she exceptionally good at what she does? Have we seen her do something kind or thoughtful? Does he love his kids? His dog? Have we seen her refuse to commit an act, however small, against her personal code of honor?

Have you shown the reader all these traits in the pages before the inciting incident? You can keep demonstrating admirable characteristics, but it's important that we admire and sympathize with your character in those early pages.

As your story progresses, it's important to have conflicted characters. In *Twilight*, Edward loves Bella and wants to preserve her life, but he also wants desperately to drink her blood. Can't get any more conflicted than that.

As your story progresses, what strong opposite desires does your protagonist exhibit? He could, for instance, listen to the voice of reason more than the voice of passion, or vice versa. Is there a point at which he is tempted to change his mind and pursue the opposite inclination?

Most readers expect to meet the protagonist in the first scene. It's jarring to read a book's chapter two and realize that *another* character is actually the protagonist. If you absolutely *must* open your story in the point of view of a character who is not your protagonist—for instance, in a thriller, where you want to open from the killer's point of view—can you move that scene to a prologue or chapter two? in order to avoid jarring the reader?

In many suspense novels, a prologue opens with a dead body or a crime victim, then in the first chapter we meet the protagonist or detective going about his ordinary work. He will then get a call to come investigate the dead body or he will stumble over it on his way home.

Many beginning writers open with a prologue for all the wrong reasons. Sometimes they are providing backstory that would be much more effective at the back of the story or in your "cut materials" file. Sometimes, because writers can't think of an exciting, gripping beginning, they grab an exciting scene from the end of the book and call it a prologue.

That's a cheap trick; please don't do it. No matter how many times you've seen it done on TV.

One more thing to consider when you're evaluating characters—when you wrote your first draft, you chose a point of view. You're either telling your story in first person (I went to the store), second person (You went to the store), third person (Tom went to the store), or omniscient (Tom decided to go to the store and Mary wondered why he was there.) If you need a review on point of view, check out the *Point of View* lesson in this series.

One key to remember: try to use only one point of view character per scene.

As you go through your manuscript, ask yourself if you're using the correct point of view character for each scene. If you are using only one point of view character for the entire novel (first person often takes this approach), then the issue is moot. But if you are using two or three point of view characters, make sure you've chosen the right one.

Let's say you're writing a novel about a married couple, Ted and Becky. You're using both of them as POV characters. You want to create friction between them, but which character should relay the story—Ted or Becky?

Ask yourself who will be the most emotionally affected by the argument. Or who will make a startling decision afterward. The reader will need to know what led to that decision, right?

You could write two scenes, one from Ted's POV and one from Becky's. Like this:

Ted wasn't surprised to find Becky sitting at the kitchen counter, her gaze glued to her iPad. Dinner was not on the stove and Gus, the Labrador, hadn't been fed. How long had she been sitting there?

He dropped his briefcase on the foyer table and stepped over her robe, which she'd apparently used to wipe up the overflow from Gus's water bowl. "And what did you do today?" he asked, hearing the sharp sound of sarcasm in his voice. "Or did someone glue your rear to that chair?"

[a space break indicates a new scene]

Becky lifted her gaze and saw Ted standing by the sink, judgment in his eyes. He had to be ticked about the mess, and in a minute he'd ask if she expected him to order take out. But he didn't believe in aliens, and he would think she was insane for watching a stream of YouTube vids all afternoon.

But he didn't know about the monsters that had just visited Las Vegas. He didn't know that a dozen people, including a couple of cops, had watched in open-mouthed horror while a group of ten-foot creatures with shiny eyes abducted a pair of show girls.

"I'm not glued," she said, resentment and fear heating her face. "But at least I'm paying attention."

He harrumphed and headed toward the bedroom.

He also didn't know she had just purchased a ticket to Vegas.

If you want to hide a character's thought process from the reader, use another character's POV to relate the action in a scene. If you want to reveal, let the reader into the mind of the character whose motives you want to make clear.

Check the POV in each scene to make sure you are using this powerful tool in the best way.

Keep a Calendar

The second draft is also the time when you should check your timeline, because time can affect your plot. In Scrivener, you can simply put the date and time on the digital card for that scene; in Word you could insert a comment at the beginning of each scene with the date and time. You may find that you have people working seven days a week with no break for the weekend, or that there's no mention of Christmas in the month of December—and Christmas can be a huge complication (or positive development) in your plot. When you're noting the date and time, also mention any unusual weather —you don't want Sue and Tom to be in a snowstorm at 10 a.m. on Thursday and find Tom's mother basking in sunshine at the same time. Details are important.

Sometimes the easiest way to keep track of time is to print out a blank calendar from your computer and use it to record which scenes happen on which date. On January 1, you could write: 2 p.m.—Josh goes to hospital, and on January 10th, record that he and Mary had a big fight. This works best, of course, if your story takes place within a relatively short period—I don't think you'd want to have a decade of paper calendars on your desk. But keeping a literal calendar also helps a writer remember that sometimes story events occur on weekends and holidays, and too often we ignore those in our novels. That's a shame, because holidays come with unique pressures, and those can be useful as we consider ways to ratchet up the pressure.

Flag the Backstory Bits

Speaking of time, check each scene for *backstory*. Your protagonist's history—any character's history, for that matter—does not belong in the first act of your book. Backstory belongs at the back of the story.

Backstory is anything that happens in your story prior to current story time. It is usually introduced through entire scenes or through recollections.

If you're writing a contemporary novel and you want to reveal how the protagonist's parents met, you might write a separate scene that begins:

> In the summer of 1972, a long-haired twenty-year-old nonconformist left home to hitchhike across the country because everyone else was doing it.

You would follow that opening sentence with an entire scene in which Jeff met Martha. That's a flashback.

If you don't want to devote that much attention to how your protagonist's parents met, you might write a recollection, which is a memory inserted within a present story scene:

> John stared at his kids, who murdered and stabbed and exploded bombs without flinching, their fingers moving soundlessly over the game controller. He had grown up with simpler entertainments—Legos and toy fire trucks and a green rubber Gumby who survived everything but the microwave. But life had been less technological in his day, and so was childhood.
>
> "Gotcha!" his son yelled, nearly levitating in his excitement.
>
> John shook his head. This was probably the most exercise his kids would get all day. He and Marge never imagined their children would turn out like this.

Do you see the recollection? An easy way to spot them is to look for the *had*—*had* almost always signals a step backward in story time. Properly used, the first *had* carries the reader back in time, and the last *had* brings him back to the present.

Both recollections and complete scene flashbacks are perfectly fine, but they should occur after the first 20-25 percent of your story. Why? Because the modern reader has grown up in a video generation, and we are accustomed to forward movement. We don't want to be slowed by history, and we don't want to stop to enjoy your character's memories until we are fully invested in his situation. Exactly when that occurs probably varies from story to story and reader to reader, but if a person is at least 20 percent into the book, odds are that he's ready and willing to pause for a bit of important backstory.

You will find tons of older novels crammed with backstory at the beginning, but they were written for a different reader. You will find some current novels that have backstory in the beginning. Backstory up front is not a fatal flaw, but I can promise you this—your story will be stronger if you move that backstory to the back or cut it entirely. Ask yourself—is it crucial that my reader know this *now*? If not, move it.

Here's a writing rule worth memorizing: *only tell your reader what he needs to know when he needs to know it.* Not before.

As you work through your second draft, mark the place where your protagonist enters the special story world, right after the inciting incident. After that point, you can include backstory if needed. But do your best to eliminate the backstory before that point—look for the "hads" to help you spot it. Then cut that backstory, place it in your "cut materials" file, and pull it out only if you need it. If that material is important, you can probably make it better and stronger by placing it at a point where your character is tormented, sad, reflective, or having his bleakest moment. That's when a poignant memory has the most power. That's when the reader is ready to explore the secret your protagonist has been carrying for years.

Whatever you do, avoid the chapter two "backstory dump." Nothing marks a beginning writer faster than a ton of backstory in chapter two.

Resist Explanation

Earlier I mentioned the acronym an editor might write in your margin: RUE, or resist the urge to explain. But how can you explain what an extinct thingamajig does if you don't explain it?

To introduce and explain an unusual object or procedure, record its effect or show it in action. For instance, if my mad scientist has invented a gadget he calls a *zilm*, I would not take two paragraphs to explain what it is, though it would be simple to write a scene where he explains his invention to a colleague. If no colleague is around, I could write something like this:

> Dr. Williams checked right and left to be sure no one was watching, then he stepped into the closet that held his safe. Carefully, as not to upset the delicate balance of the treasure inside, he punched in his code, then ever-so-gently slid the tray toward him.
>
> The zilm sat on top, glowing slightly in the dim overhead light. He exhaled, as awed as ever, and the metal zingblats vibrated, filling the air with a purring sound.
>
> "Very good," he crooned, swiveling in slow motion to avoid creating a sudden movement of air that might affect the zingblats. "We must keep you in the subsonic range."

He set the tray on the kitchen counter, then picked up his harmonica. Pressing the metal edge against his lips, he blew a note at 276 megahertz. The zingblats pulsated and sang the note back to him, the zilm's liquid center expanding, rising, and falling as it breathed in the music.

Williams shifted the harmonica and played a G; the zingblats quivered and repeated the sound. The zilm's blood red center shuddered and flattened like an egg yolk on the griddle, but when Williams ran out of breath, the zilm settled back to its natural aqueous state.

He smiled. His creation thrived on music, lapped it up. How would it respond if he played Beethoven's Ninth?

He had no time to wonder. At that instant his assistant's teakettle shrieked from the stove, and the zilm responded with a violent shudder and a whimper. Then it exploded like a bloody eyeball, spattering his lab coat and fouling his glasses.

Williams sighed and wiped his face with a handkerchief. Tomorrow, without doubt, he would make certain his assistant made tea elsewhere.

How much more effective—and fun—is this than saying, "The zilm—four inches square, with a red yolk-like substance in the center, with metal serrated edges that reacted to moving air—sat in the center of the tray."

You've heard it a dozen times: *show, don't tell*. This technique works beautifully in historical novels when you want to describe an ancient weapon or practice, and in specialized fields like medicine or technology. It's common in science fiction. Show the character interacting with the practice or object that would be unfamiliar to the typical modern reader—and have fun with it.

One thing you do not want to do is create an "As you know, Bob." That happens when a character explains something to another character that the other character would already know. For instance, in the scene above, if I'd had the assistant enter and Dr. Williams explained anything the assistant would already know, the reader would intuit the explanation was really meant for *him*. And that's not a good way to reveal new information.

So as you go through the second draft, look for any titles, objects, practices, or creatures you've explained or described in block description. Highlight those explanations and descriptions, cut them, and instead write a scene where a character *shows* how he or she relates to or interacts with whatever you're trying to illustrate.

What Genre?

Now that you have a first draft, you need to make certain you are writing in the correct genre. Many beginning writers automatically assume they're writing a novel that would fit into the "general" category, but you will have a greater chance of selling your story if you put it in a specific category. Why? Because each year publishers allot a certain number of slots for genre books, and genre readers are voracious. Romance is the biggest selling category in the world, so if you really want to sell, write a romance.

But you need to know the conventions of the genre—in a romance, the guy and the girl must get together.

In a mystery, the detective must reveal who the killer or criminal is at the end.

In a thriller, the protagonist and villain must have a confrontation before the ending.

My book *A Time to Mend* is a romance. Though there is an

important medical subplot, the story's prime focus is the attraction between a doctor and a nurse and how they must overcome various obstacles—including her breast cancer—that would keep them apart.

So what genre fits *your* novel?

Below I've listed several popular genres. The best way to understand the conventions of each is to read books in your chosen genre and write the publisher to see if they have a list of conventions they expect to find in the books they publish.

Romance is the story of two people who are meant for each other and must find their way through difficulties before they can be together. Each of them usually has a wound from the past, and through their struggles they come to appreciate each other and heal their past wounds.

The **suspense** genre is popular, but you should understand the difference between a mystery and a thriller. A mystery is a "who dun it" where a detective investigates a crime, uncovers clues and red herrings, and reveals the solution to the crime at the end of the novel. A mystery is a puzzle, and the fun of reading a mystery is trying to solve the crime along with the detective.

Because **mysteries** are a game, the reader should not have complete access to the detective's thoughts and deductions—that's why many mysteries are narrated by a third party, such as Sherlock Holmes's Dr. Watson. This enables the reader to "see" the same clues Sherlock sees, but we have to be as brilliant as Sherlock to sort out the real clues, toss out the red herrings, and come up with a solution. In a mystery, we rarely have access to the criminal's thoughts, if at all. If we do, his identity is disguised.

A **thriller**, however, is not a puzzle—it's a frantic competition between a heroic protagonist (who may or may not be a cop) and a dastardly villain. These stories may be written in first or third person and will have scenes from both the hero's and the villain's point of view. The pace of a thriller increases as the hero and the villain get closer to each other and the inevitable confrontation.

At the beginning of a thriller, the villain usually has far more resources than the hero. He may be wealthy, brilliant, good-looking, or all three. He may have a lofty reason for his crimes, but underneath it all, he may simply be cruel or psychopathic.

At the beginning of a thriller, the hero may be down on his luck, laid off, struggling financially, and in the midst of breaking up with his true love. He may have lost all confidence in his heroic abilities and wonder if he's ever done anything worthwhile.

Then a crime occurs and the hero becomes involved. He takes a personal interest in the situation, and as he moves closer to the villain, the villain takes a personal interest in the hero. They set their sights on each other.

Key point: The villain will win the early rounds, but as the story progresses, his madness or villainy or greed or pride will overcome his reason and the inherent goodness of the protagonist will begin to shift events in the hero's favor. At the confrontation, you can bet the villain will land some painful blows—or kill the best friend or the dog, or hurt the hero's daughter or wife or girlfriend—but the hero's virtue and nobility will give him the strength to rise up, steady himself, and win the day.

And we will cheer him all the way.

In the movie *Braveheart*, based on the true story of William Wallace, Wallace loses his wife to the enemy. That situation would decimate many heroes in contemporary thrillers, but Wallace fights on, not only for his late wife, but for his country and his people. He finds a higher goal and remains in the struggle. (*Braveheart* is considered to be a historical story but compare the movie's structure with the structure of a thriller as outlined above. Even though Wallace dies in the end, he is victorious in his cause. Maybe we could consider *Braveheart* a thriller in kilts.)

Women's fiction usually features a female protagonist thirty or older, married or not, often with children. While this woman may have romance in her life, the primary plot is not a romance—it's a plot that involves the issues contemporary women face: dealing with children, family, aging parents, wayward husbands, and other problems. She may or may not have a career, and she may be the woman next door. Yet her problem is not ordinary and neither is she. When put to the test, she will be stressed to the breaking point, she will suffer far more than your next-door-neighbor, and the lesson she will learn changes her life forever.

It may seem odd, but parents are rarely featured in **juvenile fiction**. Why? Because the child protagonist must be the active character. He must be the one learning the lesson, making the decisions, accepting the challenges, and experiencing the bleakest moment. If a parent is always stepping in to solve the kid's problem, the story isn't going to work.

Your child protagonist should be a little bit older than the outside age of your target reader. If you're aiming for 8-10 year olds, have your protagonist be ten or eleven. Kids love to read about older kids, not younger, and while girls will happily read about boys, most boys do not like to read about girls.

Genres fall in and out of favor (**chick lit** used to be hot, now it's not), so pay a visit to your local bookstore and ask a clerk what's selling well. Study the best-seller lists. Read the books on those lists.

Many genres employ specific point of view choices, tenses, even cover designs. For instance, when chick lit was popular, the books were usually written in first person, present tense, and featured pink and green covers. Publishing is all about "brand identification," and genre books are designed similarly so readers who pick up a book in any given genre will have a good idea of what to expect.

Whew! That's a lot to think about in a second draft, isn't it? But these are the creative elements you need to flesh out to strengthen your story. You'll still flex creative muscles in later drafts, but from draft three on, you'll primarily be using the editorial side of your brain.

So work through your novel a second time, deepening your story, adding scenes as needed to fill in gaps, and working to show more elements of your characters' personalities as they move about in their story world. Consider the details—time, date, weather—as possibilities for plot events.

Working through the second draft is easier, though not necessarily faster, than working through the first. You'll probably be dealing with more words and you'll be deepening your story. By the time you've finished, you'll have a much better book.

But there's more to come.

THE THIRD DRAFT

Done with that second draft?

After you take a day or two to fix any problems that have occurred to you as you were driving, taking a shower, or loading the dishwasher, you're ready to begin the third round.

You will switch gears in this third draft—now that you know you have a solid plot structure and well-developed characters, you need to shift into editorial gear and look for weasel words that weaken your writing.

That doesn't mean that you abandon your creative brain—you'll still be writing and adding bits here and there, but the basic story should be solid.

In this pass we are going to focus on:

- Weasel words
- Mood music and sensory details
- Tension in every scene
- Character description
- Dialogue

Here we go!

Weasel Words

Mrs. Williams, my favorite English teacher, always said we should pay ourselves a quarter for every word we can cut. Briefer is better. In this draft, you should earn a stack of metaphorical quarters.

Before you begin the third draft, let's search for and mark the weasel words. You can read a full treatment of weasel words in the lesson *Track Down the Weasel Words*, but let's consider the most common: Everyone has his or her own list of overused or weak words, but here are some common varmints: *was, were, that, really, suddenly, very, just, began to, started to, there were, there was, up, down, to her feet,* etc.

Use the search/replace feature in Scrivener or Word to search for the words on your weasel words list, then tell the program to replace those words with the same word in all caps. For instance:

Search for _*was*_ (the underscore represents a space)

Replace with _*WAS*_.

Search for _*brow*

Replace with _*BROW*

When you've done that procedure for every word on your list, your manuscript will be dotted with lots of words in all caps. That's okay. The simple act of going through the manuscript to replace those words with proper capitalization will force you to evaluate: can you find a better way to say this? A more active way? Can you replace this wimpy verb with an active verb? Can you delete this word altogether?

Anyone who sits *down* or stands *up* can also sit and stand.

Very almost always needs to disappear.

Ditto for *suddenly*.

If you're brave—and I hope you are—you might want to do a search for *ly* (no space before) and replace with *LY*. This will highlight most of your adverbs, and 90 percent of them need to go. You'll be grateful when they're all lying dead on the floor.

Was/were are passive verbs and tend to create passive writing. Why write "The cat was on the table" when you could write "The cat sprawled on the table," or "the cat reclined on the table?" I'm not saying you have to delete every single *was*, but if you can replace *was* with an active verb, by all means, do. Ditto for *were*.

That is simply overused . Whenever it shows up in one of my search/replace functions, I consider the sentence without the *that*. If the sentence makes sense, I cut it.

It is another weasel word. There are okay *its* and not okay *its*, and usage makes the difference. If I write, "She wore a blue skirt with flowers on it," the reader has no trouble realizing that the *it* refers to the skirt. But if I write, "*It* is hard to get a driver's license," to what does that *it* refer? That's imprecise writing, and you can do better. So whenever you see a nebulous *it*, back up and start over, writing exactly what you mean: "Getting a driver's license is complicated."

Individual writers have personal weasel words. I tend to overuse smiles and eyebrows, so while I'm not going to completely avoid them, I will try to limit myself to one smile and/or one eyebrow gyration per page.

Make a list of *your* weasel words and get into the habit of tagging them. Your manuscript will thank you.

Other words are so obvious they are unnecessary.

He clapped ~~his hands~~. How else would he clap?

She nodded ~~in approval~~. A nod *means* approval.

He climbed ~~up~~ the stairs. If you're climbing stairs, you're going up.

~~*He shook his head.*~~ *"No, I won't do that."* His head shake reveals his noncompliance.

She threw up her hands. That's gross.

He sat and drank his coffee with a jerk. Who was the jerk?

His heart thumped ~~in his chest.~~ Only an alien's heart would thump elsewhere . . .

She rose ~~to her feet.~~ What else would she rise to?

He caught her eye. Did she intend to throw it? (Okay, that one is fairly colloquial, but still . . .)

She rolled her eyes. Like a pair of dice?

When we are "in the zone" writing, when the words flow from our fingertips, it's easy for all kinds of unnecessary weasels to slip onto the page. This draft—and succeeding drafts—gives you the opportunity to catch and kill them before they clutter and weaken your story.

Mood Music

When you consider a scene, ask yourself what sort of music would be playing in the background if this scene were a movie. Fast or slow? Loud or soft? Once you've determined that, try to create that music through words.

For instance, if the scene is fast paced, use shorter and more active sentences.

> He'd been seen. John vaulted over the wall and blasted through the alley. Thunder boomed in the distance as hail pelted his neck. Run. Run. Dive.

If, however, you want to stretch out a moment, make your sentences longer, almost never-ending.

Why would you want to slow down story time? Sometimes a crucial story event happens too quickly—a gunshot, a car crash, a lightning strike. When a quick event is important to the story and to your protagonist, you need to s-t-r-e-t-c-h that moment, and you do it by breaking every rule you've ever heard about run-on sentences.

He saw the gun, the muzzle flash, and felt the sharp pain at his gut before his ears rang with the sound, but what was it they told him in medical school, that bullets were supersonic, that they did more damage going in than most people realized, and that what we saw on TV was laughable, even a .30 caliber bullet would carve a hole in a man's middle before landing against his spine, or, worse yet, blasting through him and gutting some poor innocent bystander who happened to be in the way or standing by the elevator or waiting for his pregnant wife to bring their first child into the world . . .

By writing something like the paragraph above, you have slowed the speed of a supersonic bullet to as long as it takes a reader to read that run-on sentence.

If you're writing a tense scene, set it on a dark and stormy night. I know it sounds cliche, but cliches are cliches for a reason. What you *shouldn't* do is use the words "dark and stormy night." Instead, show it, don't tell it. Write in a branch scraping across a windowpane or having wind moan outside the house.

I'm getting ready to start a book in which the Great Fire of Rome plays an important role. I will foreshadow the event by mentioning the hot, turbulent wind in the days preceding the event, and may mention the acrid smell of smoke rising from the multi-story wooden structures that crowded the valleys of Rome. I want readers to be able to feel the heat and smell meat sizzling on braziers.

Another thing you can do to set the mood is look for anything in a scene that involves the senses: seeing, hearing, tasting, touching, smelling, or intuiting. Try to include at least three sensory references in every scene. These details will help your reader feel that he is right in the thick of your story.

It's easy to write what characters *see*, but don't forget about what they *hear*. Let your character run her hand over a velvet robe or *taste* the bitter tang of an herbal leaf. Let her enter a room and shiver with a premonition . . . your reader will shiver, too.

Pump Up the Emotion

Another thing to consider as you evaluate each scene is the level of emotion. When I first started writing, I often heard that I needed to portray more emotion. I get it—I'm as emotional as the next woman, but I'm more of a thinker than a feeler. I tended to write things like:

She stared at him. "I'm mad!"

Well, maybe I wasn't *quite* that on the nose, but my novels were long on thought and short on emotion. But why do people read fiction? To *feel*. If they want facts, they'll read nonfiction. People read novels because they want to live vicariously in your protagonist's skin.

So when Jane's husband leaves her, you can't have Jane shrug and go into the kitchen for a cup of tea. You need to place us in Jane's head and heart so we know what she's thinking and we feel what she's feeling.

I explained how to do this in the *Evoking Emotion* lesson, so I won't repeat all of that information here. But if something horrific or wonderful or amazing or frightening has happened to your character, make sure the reader has the opportunity to feel those emotions, too. And resist the urge to show emotion through exclamation marks. That particular piece of punctuation should be like hot peppers—used in moderation, if at all. We have to show emotion through words, images, and metaphors.

As you go through your novel this third time, look at each scene as a detached unit. If your character is reeling from a setback, ask yourself if you're fully exploring that emotion. Not every scene has to involve major drama, and sometimes emotion is best expressed through understatement and subtext. Make sure your reader has the opportunity to feel that emotion, even if your character suppresses it.

An actor friend of mine told me that one way an actor can get the audience to cry is by obviously choking back an emotion—the audience will cry or gasp instead. That's also a handy writer's trick.

Remember that emotion is rarely pure—love, for instance, is comprised of jealousy, joy, sorrow, and happiness, just to name a few typical feelings. A grieving person moves through shock, denial, anger, bargaining, depression, and finally, acceptance. I'll never forget the day I called a friend whose daughter had just been killed—we were both stunned, we both wept, and from out of nowhere, she said something funny and we laughed. When tragedy strikes, emotions swirl without rhyme or reason.

When something important happens in your story, your characters are likely to be caught up in an emotional whirlwind, so be sure your characters go through every emotion that suits their personalities.

Do your characters experience only one note of an emotion, or do you portray the true richness of an emotional experience? If something happens to your character, they may not truly feel the emotion until the *next* scene. Some writers create stories in an action/reaction pattern. That's fine, but don't let that pattern dominate your entire novel.

Tension in Every Scene

As you go through your third draft, make sure there is

some kind of tension on each page. I'm not saying your characters have to argue in every scene. Tension could result in an argument or fight, of course, but tension could also be something that tells us your character is uneasy. Look for any scenes where your character is doing nothing but sitting and thinking, traveling, or drinking coffee.

If your character needs to think, travel, or have a cup of coffee, make sure his thoughts are unsettling. Raise troubling memories or questions in his mind, and you will also raise them in the reader's . . . and that will keep the reader reading until he or she learns the answer to those questions.

But if you've written a scene where Mrs. Jones and Mrs. Smith are pleasantly drinking tea and discussing the weather, reconsider, especially if the scene goes on for pages. Instead, let Mrs. Smith make a cutting remark that wounds Mrs. Jones, but Mrs. Jones is too polite to remonstrate. Then let Mrs. Jones think about all the ways Mrs. Smith has hurt her over the years, and how she could seek revenge . . . even as she smiles and says, "Would you like cream with that?"

The reader will keep reading because she wants to see if Mrs. Jones will actually do something to Mrs. Smith. That's tension. And you should make sure every page has it.

Check your dialog to be sure it corresponds with the age, rank, and social status of the speaker. I've read many a well-intentioned manuscript written about a child who talks like an adult. If you're going to write in a child's or teenager's point of view, it's imperative that you spend some time with children or teens of the appropriate age. Learn their language, but don't overdose on their slang. Slang changes quickly, and if you incorporate too much, your book will be dated in no time. Instead, learn speech patterns. Study how children and teens think, and spend time talking to kids. Then you'll be better prepared to write realistic dialogue.

Always remember that dialogue is not actual speech—it's an *approximation* of actual speech. When you meet a friend, you may exchange five minutes of nothing but small talk, the usual "how are you?" and "What have you been up to?" You may tell your friend a story you told your mother the day before, then you'll share whatever's on your heart.

When you're writing dialogue, don't waste time on small talk. You can say they greeted each other, then jump straight to the point. And don't have one character tell another the story he told someone else five pages ago. You can summarize ("After telling her about my stolen wallet . . .") or just have the friend say, "You're kidding, someone stole your wallet?"

Weasel words, by the way, catch a break in dialogue. People don't always speak with proper grammar, so let your characters use all the weasel words if it feels natural. A college professor probably wouldn't speak so carelessly, but a teenage kid might. Let your dialogue be a natural approximation of real speech.

If you're writing a foreign character, feel free to sprinkle a few words of his native language through your manuscript, but make sure the foreign word's meaning in clear in context. Standard practice is to italicize the foreign word the first time you use it, but not thereafter.

One way to make a character sound as though English is not his first language is simply to eliminate all contractions. This naturally results in stilted, more formal speech.

I use that technique when writing about ancient times. Since my ancient Roman, Greek, or Egyptian characters didn't speak English, everything I write is a translation. But if my characters' dialogue is too relaxed and conventional, readers say it sounds too modern. Eliminating the contractions adds an air of formality that conveys the feeling of an ancient speaker.

While you're examining your dialogue, consider your use

of profanity. From reading reviews on Amazon.com, I've learned that lots of readers enjoy "clean" because it doesn't rattle their senses with offensive language.

Rough language makes a lot of people uncomfortable. That statement is probably a little less true with every passing year, but anything that breaks the "fictive dream" for a reader weakens the story, and profanity is one of the things that can interrupt a reader's reading experience.

When I am writing characters who would and do use profanity, I will usually write something like "he turned the air blue with expletives" or "he cursed."

Writing dialogue with profanity is easy. Finding a way to impart that same flavor and information without profanity is a challenge. But it's a challenge worth accepting if you can hook the reader with your story.

If you don't want to avoid profanity completely, consider that there are mildly offensive words and highly offensive words. And while most people don't mind reading the mildly offensive words, they can become extremely annoyed when a book for which they paid good money contains language that make them want to toss the book in the trash.

Just sayin'.

Check the physical descriptions of your characters.

How much physical description of a character is needed? The answer may depend on genre. Romance readers tend to like detailed descriptions; other readers prefer to visualize characters in their own heads. I don't insert much physical description other than mentioning hair and eye color if and when appropriate. Sometimes a physical characteristic is part of someone's character—for example, a man called "Hare" who comes up to his fellow gladiator's elbow. That's really all I need to say.

But if you need to describe a character, start with the larger picture and focus. Don't give us an entire paragraph of block description but sprinkle descriptive details through the character's actions.

This *used* to be the standard way to describe a character:

> John Lee stood near the door, all six foot three inches of him, dressed in Levi's and a plaid cowboy shirt. Dolly noted that his broad chest and strong arms lay beneath a sharply chiseled face. That strong jaw, that classic nose were truly noteworthy, but those blue eyes were unforgettable.

Today's reader doesn't want the action to stop for description. The following is a better way to describe a character—it's more active. Notice though, that both descriptions begin with his overall impression—height—and move to focus on the most compelling aspect of this person, his eyes. Begin macro, finish micro.

> John Lee strode into the room, dwarfing the knot of less-statuesque men huddled around the punch bowl. He walked over to the guestbook, his cowboy boots clunking on the wooden floor, and wiped his hands on his blue jeans before picking up a pen to sign the register.
>
> Dolly felt her gaze rove over his broad shoulders, and her throat tightened when he looked up and caught her watching him. His classic nose crinkled when he smiled, and his unforgettable blue eyes sparked with interest . . .

Work through your manuscript, scene by scene, evaluating each for weasel words, mood music, sensory details, tension, character description, and dialogue. When you're done, take a couple of days for triage, reworking any scenes that just don't quite feel right yet.

Then come back and get ready for draft four.

THE FOURTH DRAFT

Take a couple of days for triage after you've completed your third draft. If you've made notes to yourself in sidebars or comment balloons, go back and fix or incorporate whatever is needed.

Then print out your manuscript, settle back in your easy chair, and grab a pen or marker with brightly colored ink. This fourth draft offers a delicious change of pace because you're going to use your ears.

In this draft, work through the novel again, scene by scene. Read through it silently, cut and tighten and deepen as you can—and then ask the computer to read the edited scene. Both Scrivener and Word have options that allow you to highlight text (in this case, the entire scene), and the computer will read it to you.

Why not read the manuscript aloud yourself? You can, but your eye will probably gloss over the typos you've been glossing over all along. You are also likely to read dramatically, inserting the emotion you felt as you wrote.

As the computer reads, listen with a printed copy of your

third draft in hand. The slightly robotic voice is a benefit, because the words must carry the emotion, as opposed to the voice in your head. Follow along on the text and mark anything that clunks against your ear.

What will create a clunking sound?

Repetition, sometimes called an "echo:" *She stared at him as he went down the stairs.* Your eye may not see that *stared* and *stairs* sound the same, but your ear will recognize that it sounds off-putting. So change the *stairs* to *steps*.

Whenever I hear an echo or repeated sound, I circle the repeated words and write "rep" in the margin. Sometimes I'll realize that I've used the same word three times in one paragraph, so I'll circle all of them. The more distinctive the word, the more it will stand out.

Sometimes listening will help you realize that you've only given a couple of lines—only seconds in listening time—to explore a major character epiphany that needs more than a few lines to develop. Or perhaps the opposite is true—your character may be musing over something, and they keep thinking and thinking and thinking while nothing of interest is happening on the page.

Sometimes names clunk against the ear. In a recent book I had two characters named Narkis and Marcus. Not a problem, until I heard them used together: *Narkis threw Marcus a sharp look.*

Uh oh. The cute rhyme was not at all what I intended. I made certain Marcus and Narkis were never again mentioned in the same sentence.

Listen for too many *saids* or *body movements*.

"I don't know what's going on," he said.
   "I don't know, either," she said.
   "Maybe they're out of town," he said.

"You may be right," she said.

He propped his chin in his hand. "I saw the dog outside last night."

She scratched her nose. "Was he loose?"

He shrugged. "Maybe. Who knows?"

Said is a perfectly fine word. It's practically invisible, unless you pile it up in stanzas like the exchange above. Likewise, there's nothing wrong with body movements, often called *beats*, to break up an exchange in dialogue, but don't use them in a consistent pattern.

Much better to edit like this:

"I don't know what's going on," Tom said.

Mary frowned. "I don't know, either."

"Maybe they're out of town?"

"Maybe—but Susan didn't mention a trip."

"Wait." He propped his chin in his hand. "I saw the dog outside last night."

"Was he running loose?"

"I couldn't tell. Who knows?"

When you're considering sections of dialogue, watch those speaker attributions—usually, a simple *said* is best if something is needed. Avoid having people exclaim, scream, roar, yell, chortle, snicker, or smile (you can't *smile* words).

And if you have even one adverb in a speaker attribution —"Right," he said *snarkily*—cut it. Writers use adverbs when they can't find a stronger verb, and you can do better putting the snark in the *words*, not in a writerly comment on the character's speech. The writer should be as invisible as possible so the story can shine.

So use your fourth draft to listen to your manuscript.

After you've gone through a chapter or a scene, turn back to your computer and enter your changes. If you've made major edits to a paragraph or scene, listen to it again to make sure the changes flow. There is a rhythm to language, and when it sounds right, it usually is.

In this fourth draft, watch out for **plot strings**. What's a plot string? It's a plot change that might affect other scenes in the book. Maybe it's a small change and maybe it's big, but when making changes in the third and fourth draft, a writer must be careful not to pull a string and cause holes throughout the rest of the book.

For instance, in my first draft of *Bathsheba* I decided that she would come to love King David after the death of their first son.

But later I realized that I was missing a great opportunity for conflict if I let her love him right away—after all, the timeline of the book ranged from David's kingship until Solomon's, a long time. And Bathsheba had lots of reasons *not* to love David—he was an inattentive father, he surrendered seven of Saul's sons to the Gibeonites for execution, he forced himself on her when they first met, and he had her husband murdered. Plenty of reasons for her to resist loving the king, right?

So I made the change in one pivotal scene, then I had to go through the entire book to evaluate Bathsheba's thoughts and feelings about David. She needed an attitude shift, and she needed it in nearly all of her point of view scenes.

So if you pull one string in your tightly constructed plot, you must make sure you haven't created inconsistencies in the rest of the story. Making changes at this stage isn't easy, but it's possible and often advisable.

The Theme of Your Story

At its core, what is your story *about*? I'll be honest—I often don't know what my theme is until the third or fourth draft. At that point, I go back through the manuscript and drop in hints and symbols that echo or refer to the theme.

Was *Breaking Bad* about a dying man trying to provide for his family or about how pride can destroy a man's life? Walter White, chemistry teacher, tells himself that his decision to cook methamphetamine is to provide for his family, but when he reaches a point where his family is secure, he can't quit his criminal sideline because he doesn't want to. He's the best cook in the business, and pride goads him forward. When another man associated with the production of methamphetamine is killed and Walt's ATF agent brother-in-law says the dead guy must be the mythical genius for which the ATF has been searching, Walt can't resist saying, "Really? He couldn't have been that smart."

Walt becomes an illustration of how *pride goes before a fall*.

Your theme could be about justice, or true love, or sacrifice, or honor. Every novel has a message, even if subtly presented, and it's the principle you are illustrating for your reader. It's the reader takeaway.

What is your novel about? Look beyond what your character is doing on the page and ask yourself why he's doing it. What is his motivation? Is he motivated by a desire to save the world? His family? Or is he only serving himself? What are you, the author, trying to tell the world through this story?

Is your protagonist risking everything in order to make a million bucks or because he loves his family? Is she flirting with a man at work because she's unhappy in her marriage or because she's afraid she's no longer young and beautiful?

Clarify your character's external and internal motivations.

Most characters freely admit their external motivation—Walter White was happy to say he was trying to provide for his family, but would have been reluctant to admit the internal reason for his actions. Write a scene where your protagonist is forced to verbalize the truth about his or her *why*, and you'll be illustrating your theme.

Odds and Ends

Names: People rarely use each other's names in dialog. My husband and I recently discovered the Jesse Stone movies, starring Tom Selleck. We really like them, but we couldn't help noticing that the characters constantly refer to each other by name:

> "I don't know, Jesse. What do you think?"
> "I think he could be the killer, Glenda."
> "Really, Jesse?"
> "Really, Glenda."

That's not the actual dialogue, but you get the point. After a while, the effect becomes comical. If you intend to do that on purpose, okay. But if not, look through your manuscript and see if your characters are constantly using the other person's name in dialogue. Nine times out of ten, the name shouldn't be there.

The FAS principle: whenever you have a sentence with the elements of emotion, action, and speech, but them in this order: Feeling, then action, then speech.

Let's say that James feels a rush of gratitude. He hugs Martha, who has just given him a gift. He says "thank you."

Now consider the order:

"Thank you!" James hugged Martha and felt a rush of gratitude.

OR

James hugged Martha. "Thank you!" He felt a rush of gratitude.

OR

Feeling a rush of gratitude, James hugged Martha. "Thank you!"

Feelings come first, then action, then speech. Any other order feels slightly off.

The pencil principle: the most important part of a sentence or the most compelling argument in a list should always be at the end. Think of a pencil: the most important part—the point—is at the end. The second most important part—the eraser—is at the beginning. So if your sentence contains three elements, put the most important part at the end, the second most important part at the beginning, and the supporting words in the middle.

Example: She would always love him—he was her son, her joy, her life.

OR She would always love him—he was her joy, her life, her son.

The first sentence implies that she's a smother mother. The second depicts a normal mother-son relationship.

Phonetic spellings: avoid phonetic spellings in your dialogue except for the occasional dropped *g* in something like "dreamin' of a white Christmas." Far better to indicate someone's foreign or unusual speech by word choice. Whatever you write, make sure it's easy to read.

In her amazing bestseller (eleven million copies!) *The Help*, Kathryn Stockett does a great job of creating the speech of a black woman from Mississippi with word choice. Here's her first paragraph:

Mae Mobley was born on a early Sunday morning in August 1960. A church baby we like to call it. Taking care a white babies, that what I do, along with all the cooking and the cleaning. I done raised seventeen kids in my lifetime. I know how to get them babies to sleep, stop crying, and go to the toilet before they mamas even get out a bed in the morning.[1]

Notice that the passage above isn't dialogue, it's the voice of our protagonist, Abileen. We are firmly in her head, and her distinctive voice helps establish who she is.

Compare that to this passage from Margaret Mitchell's bestseller, *Gone With the Wind*. Mitchell's book has also sold millions of copies, but it was first published in 1936, a far different time.

"Ef you doan care 'bout how folks talks 'bout dis family, Ah does," [Mammy] rumbled. "Ah ain' gwine stand by an' have eve'body at de party sayin' how you ain' botched up right. Ah has tole you an' tole you dat you kin allus tell a lady by dat she eat lak a bird. An' Ah ain' aimin' ter have you go ter Mist' Wilkes' an' eat lak a fe'el han' an' gobble lak a hawg."[2]

If Ms. Mitchell were writing today, I think she'd write that passage this way: "If you don't care about how folks talks about this family, I does," Mammy said. "I ain't goin' stand by and have ever body at the party sayin' how you ain't brought up right. I has told you and told you that you can always tell a lady 'cause she eat like a bird. I ain't aimin' to have you go to Mister Wilkes' and eat like a field hand and gobble like a hog."

Same effect, but *much* easier to read. So if you want to

establish a unique voice or accent, study the word patterns of that accent and use those.

I've written a handful of books set in Ireland, and I've been delighted to visit that country three times. Each time, I kept a notebook and jotted down unique phrases that were part of everyday speech. With a list of those phrases, I was able to make my Irish characters sound authentic without resorting to strange spellings.

Stream of Consciousness writing is when the writer records every thought running through a point of view character's mind. Use this technique only when the character is sick, drunk, or otherwise mentally impaired. Avoid this technique at other times, as it can become wearying for your reader.

Naming characters: Incidental characters such as the newspaper boy, the postal carrier, and the taxi driver do not need names unless they play an important role in the story. Readers don't like having to keep up with too many named characters.

Telling is not always bad: If the information is part of a longer list of information or history, tell it. If this information will cause a reaction in your protagonist, show it.

If I were writing a murder mystery involving an old trunk, I'd *tell*:

Glenda undid the lock and took inventory: The trunk contained a vintage dress, a bundle of faded love letters, and several packets of old Simplicity sewing patterns.

If I were writing a novel of women's fiction, I'd *show*:

Glenda shoved aside the vintage dress and the bundle of faded love letters, but her heart skipped a beat when she spied a packet of sewing patterns, circa 1952. There it was, the dress. The one her mother had worn in the yellowed photograph. The one in which she'd been holding another baby, a baby who wasn't Glenda.

Scene Structure

In this fourth draft, you'll want to spend extra time on the **beginnings and endings** of scenes. Scenes should end with a punchy line, almost a verbal equivalent of *ba da dum*. Scenes should open with a strong sentence, too, a line that lets the reader know who the point of view character is.

Remember: to prevent reader confusion, only have one point of view character per scene.

Each scene should be anchored in a specific time and place. A scene may open with a bit of third person narrative, but by the end of that scene, the reader should feel as if he or she knows *where* the POV character is and *when* the scene is taking place.

Example: Tom Jones stared into the bright lights of the stage and wondered how many times he had sung "She's a Lady."

When the sentence opens, the camera is *outside* Mr. Jones's head, so that's a wee bit of third person. But by the time the reader reaches the word *wondered*, we have moved into Jones's head. We should stay there until the end of the scene.

So in this draft, check the beginning and ending of each scene. Does the scene open with a strong line? Does it close with something punchy? The scene should not end as if you simply ran out of things to say.

Is the scene set in a certain time and place? You should be able to chart all your scenes on a timeline and give each a date, time, and location.

Sometimes you want to open with a bit of narrative that

covers a longer period of time. That's fine, but conclude that scene with action anchored in a specific time and place.

Here's an example from the ending of *Bathsheba*:

[Narrative] Nine years passed—years in which David, my lord and king and husband, grew old. From his wives and concubines he no longer sought pleasure, but warmth, yet we were growing old with him. To better care for the aging king, one of his servants suggested that the palace seek out a young woman, a virgin, who would become his handmaid. She would care for him, feed him, and sleep with him to keep him warm.

. . .

[set time and place] "The prophet Nathan," my servant told me, "waits for you in the palace garden."

. . .

I pulled my veil over my graying hair and hurried outside, then slipped up the stairs to the elevated garden. Nathan sat in a shady alcove, but he rose and bowed when he saw me.

. . .

[Ending of scene] And the Lord sent Nathan, who told me what must be done.

"I am only doing this because I believe it is Adonai's will," I told the prophet. Then I lifted my chin and led the way out of the garden.

In each of your scenes, will the reader realize who the point of view character is by the time he's read the first or second sentence? Some books use external devices to handle this problem, especially if the book is written in first person so each character refers to himself as "I." The POV character's name may be a heading in each chapter, for instance, or the character scenes may be typeset in different fonts.

Your Novel's Beginning and Ending

After you have listened to and adjusted your fourth draft, go back to pay special attention to your novel's beginning and ending.

Let's start at the top.

Your first line is probably the most important sentence in your novel. Why? Because you only have a few seconds to hook your reader. Browsers in a bookstore see the spine first, then the cover, then they might flip the book over to skim the back cover copy. If all those things have piqued their interest, they will then open the book and read your first line—so it had better be the best line in the novel.

If your potential buyer is browsing online, they'll click on the preview, skip the front matter, and read that first sentence—and you'd better hook them, or they'll be off to look for another book among the millions of available titles.

The First Fifty Pages lesson discusses this in detail, but here's the summary of how to have a winning first sentence: make sure your first sentence has a person (because we enjoy reading about people more than reading about weather, furniture, landscapes, or galaxies far, far away) and something that raises a provocative question.

The best first line I ever read was from *Second Glance*, a Jodi Picoult novel. Her opening sentence was this: "Ross Wakeman succeeded the first time he tried to kill himself, but not the second or the third."

Does your first sentence work as well as *that* one?

When I teach, I have my students write their first sentences on a slip of paper, then pass them to me. Under the cover of anonymity, I read each of the sentences aloud and ask the class to respond in one of three ways. If they were totally hooked and would keep reading, they are to raise their hands high. If they might keep reading, they raise their hands about shoulder height. And if the sentence didn't grab them, they don't raise their hands at all.

It's always a revealing exercise, as writers who thought they had a good opening realize it isn't as strong as they'd hoped.

Even something like, "Oh no! He was going to kill her!" can be dull because 1) it feels cliché and 2) we don't know who's saying this, so we don't care. When opening with dialogue, unless the quote is so clever that it has to be coming from an intelligent and fascinating character, it can fall flat.

So if you've written:

Julie Smith opened her eyes and knew she was in trouble.

The reader has one question in her mind: Why is she in trouble?

So try this instead:

Julie Smith opened her eyes into darkness and felt the slick satin of cheap casket lining beneath her fingertips.

Now the reader has *lots* of questions: How'd she get in a casket? How'd she *know* she was in a casket? Did someone bury her alive? Does she sleep in a casket like one of the undead? Has someone tried to kill her or is she the victim of an inexperienced doctor? She probably works in a mortuary, because she's quick to identify that "slick satin" with a "cheap casket."

See how a few details can raise several provocative questions in the reader's mind? The reader will keep reading because once we think of a question, we naturally want to know the answer.

That's what you want. That's how you keep people reading from page to page.

You would not want to say:

> Julie Smith opened her eyes and felt the slick satin of a cheap casket beneath her fingertips, then wailed because her evil stepfather had finally carried out his threats to kill her for the insurance money.

That sentence gives the reader too much information. Any question we might have thought of is answered before the sentence ends—except maybe, "Can she escape?"

Your task in the first sentence—indeed, the first chapter—is to give enough information to arouse interest, not to explain every detail.

But be careful—I've read some manuscripts that gave so little information that I was confused. If your reader can't tell what's going on, they may put the book down. People read for entertainment, so if a book is too much work, why not watch TV?

So in this draft, read your first sentence. Does it contain a person? Does it give us details that raise a provocative question in the reader's mind? If your first sentence doesn't work, play around with it until it does. Or start over.

Write several variations of your opening line, then try them out on impartial friends. Which one hooks their interest best?

Now that you've written an irresistible first line, take a long look at your last sentence and last paragraph. In chapter one, you were trying to hook the reader's interest. In your last chapter, you are aiming to deliver an emotional punch that will resonate long after the reader puts the book down.

How do you do that?

Consider echoing the theme of the story. You have settled on a theme, so how can you restate or illustrate it in your ending?

Some of the most powerful endings bring the story full circle by repeating an element from the beginning of the story. The character may be in the same place, thinking the same thoughts, or seeing the same view, but now he or she is deeply changed, so those thoughts, that view, are seen and felt from a different perspective.

What is happening at the beginning of your story? Where is your protagonist? What is he thinking and/or viewing? Is there any way you can include some of these elements in your ending?

Example: my novel *Bathsheba* opens like this:

> According to family history, when my parents presented me to Samuel at the time of my mother's purification, the Ruach HaKodesh touched the ordinarily eloquent prophet in such a way that the torrent of words from his lips resembled nothing so much as a stream of gibberish . . .
>
> At only eighty days old, I retained no memory of my encounter with the prophet, but in the years ahead I came to understand that a river of foretellings and curses had carved out the events of my life, a torrent of words with the power to rip me from people I loved and settle me on unexpected shores.

My novel closed like this:

> I am now a woman of more than seventy years. I have known great sorrow, and I have known great joy. But throughout the winding length of my life, I have been pulled and directed by words that sprang from prophets' lips after being breathed by the Ruach HaKodesh.
>
> And I am content.

Examine your novel's ending, and see if you can incorporate the theme, an element from the beginning, your beginning location, or the ideas from your first chapter into your ending.

If you've come with me this far, you have made really great progress!

---

1. Kathryn Stockett, THE HELP, New York: Berkley, 2011.
2. Margaret Mitchell, GONE WITH THE WIND, New York: McMillan, 1936.

THE FIFTH DRAFT

You have spent at least two drafts writing and fleshing out your story. You have spent at least two drafts self-editing your story. Now it's time to add a bit of polish that will help your manuscript look more professional.

Use the search/replace function of your word processor to search for [space, space] and replace with [space]. And because spaces are invisible, you should put your cursor in the search box and hit the space bar two times. Then put your cursor in the replace box and hit it once. Repeat as many times as needed until you have no double spaces in your manuscript.

When students took typing classes, they were taught to separate sentences with two spaces, and that habit dies hard with a lot of folks—and sometimes extra spaces creep into our documents. Doing this search and replace will ferret them out.

Search for any **ellipses.** Though some word processors are set to automatically replace . . . with [dot dot dot], the correct way to use them is [space dot space dot space dot.]

You rarely need to use four dots in fiction because they pertain to quoted reference material.

You can use an ellipsis when someone takes a poignant pause in dialogue: "You know . . . I thought he loved me."

Or you can use them when someone trails off in thought: "I knew a lad like Billy once . . ."

Do not use ellipses when someone is interrupted in dialogue. That calls for an em dash (hyphen hyphen, which most word processors immediately replace with a long dash).

"Get out of here, you lazy—"

Search for your **exclamation points** and replace almost all of them with a period. Keep them only if someone is screaming for help . . . or on fire. Maybe. Nothing marks an amateur manuscript faster than an overdose of exclamation marks.

If you haven't already done so, consider adding a **symbol** to your story. What is an object that can represent something significant to your protagonist? Write it into the beginning or middle of the story, then mention it again at the end of your novel . . . and let the reader see how your changed protagonist views this symbol in a different way.

In my novel *Doesn't She Look Natural*, Jen is newly divorced, and she wants to reconcile with her husband. She keeps her wedding rings in a box in her bureau, and at least once in the story she pulls them out to try them on, praying that she'll be wearing them again soon.

Then her ex-husband shows up to tell her he's marrying his girlfriend, and the news devastates Jen. But as he's leaving, his car is involved in an auto accident and he's killed. Jen, who has heretofore hated all things funereal, goes to the mortuary to slip her wedding band onto her deceased husband's pinky finger. She's saying goodbye to him, but more important, she's finally able to say goodbye to her wedding ring . . . and the dream of restoring her marriage.

Can you think of an object in your story that can be imbued with emotional significance and mentioned at least twice in the course of your story's events?

Don't forget the **spell and grammar check**. Nearly every word processing program has one, so use it well.

Remember that the grammar check's strict approach may not apply to a novel. In a novel, characters speak with bad grammar, they stutter, they use run on sentences. So don't let your grammar checker be overly legalistic in your characters' dialogue.

Consider an **author's note** at the end. If you've taken liberties with geography or historical timelines, or if you'd like to thank the professionals you interviewed for your character's occupation, write an author's note in which you speak directly to the reader. Generously praise the folks who helped you out, mentioning them by name, and be sure to spell their names correctly. Don't forget that last important line: "If there are any errors in my depiction of a herpetologist (or whatever), the mistakes are mine alone."

If you think a book club might enjoy discussing your novel, consider including **discussion questions**. People who lead book clubs appreciate authors who write discussion questions for the back of the book. I've led a book club for years, and feedback from those intelligent readers has helped me grow as a writer—and no, we don't discuss my books.

Even if the average reader doesn't belong to a book club, discussion questions can help your reader explore some of the ideas you've presented in your story. So go ahead and come up with ten or twelve questions for your novel. They just might prompt a reader to suggest your novel for the next meeting of her book club.

If your novel required a lot of research, you might want to consider a **bibliography**. Most novelists don't include a bibliography, but when I rely heavily on other people's books and articles, I want to give them credit. Plus, some readers may be so fascinated by a concept that they'd like to read more about it, so a book list would be appreciated. Adding a bibliography doesn't hurt anything, and it may help prove that you did your homework, especially if you're writing about a complicated topic or historical era.

Consider a **note to your reader**, inviting him or her to leave a review on Amazon.com or other retail website. This is a relatively new idea, but certainly worth investigating, especially if you are self-publishing. Publishing is not what it was ten years ago, and most authors, even those who are traditionally published, find themselves responsible for most of their own marketing. So why not ask your reader to share a review if they enjoyed the story?

Check your **manuscript formatting**. Your manuscript should be formatted in the traditional manner—no fancy fonts, no colored inks, no odd layouts. If you are sending the manuscript off to an agent or publisher, you should lay it out for an 8.5 x 11 page with one-inch margins at the sides and bottom. Allow a 1.5 inch margin at the top. Double space. Begin a new chapter on a new page. Use a standard font like Garamond or Times New Roman. Make sure the font is 11 or 12 point—any smaller and you'll strain the editor's eyes.

Your name and address should be in the upper left corner. You might want to add the manuscript's word count beneath the page number in the upper right corner.

The title should be in the center of the middle of the page, with your byline beneath it. (Hint: don't write "by Your Name." Just write "Your Name.")

If you have an agent, place his or her name, address, and phone number in the bottom right corner of the title page.

Formatting details aren't nearly as important today as they were before everything went digital. Fonts and sizing can now be changed with a couple of keystrokes, so this emphasis on proper formatting may seem trivial.

But if you use the proper formatting, an editor will **know that you know** how formatting should be done. If you use bizarre formatting, your manuscript will reek of inexperience.

Check your **chapter breaks**. Big shifts of time and/or place deserve a chapter break. Depending on your story, insert a chapter break every 15-20 pages, so the reader has a nice stopping place.

But sometimes you should do the opposite. You can insert a chapter break at a tense moment to entice your reader to begin another chapter. If you do this, however, make sure the next scene and chapter do *not* pick up where you left off—instead, insert a scene from another character's point of view to stretch out the tension a little bit longer.

When you've taken care of all these details (and any others that have occurred to you), your manuscript is ready to send to a "beta reader." If you are publishing traditionally, this is optional because your editor will give you feedback. But if you are self-publishing, I'd strongly urge you to find at least two good test readers. These folks are not editors—you're going to ask them to read for pleasure, not work.

THE BETA READERS

A beta reader is not a *first* reader; think of him or her as a *test* reader. Just as software companies release beta copies of new programs for people to try, you can give your nearly-completed manuscript to a beta reader for constructive feedback.

But choose your beta reader(s) carefully. You don't want to give your manuscript to your relative or friend who won't be honest about your work. You should find a beta reader who reads a lot in your chosen genre—if you've written a murder mystery, you don't want to give it to a cousin who thinks *Law and Order* is too violent.

If you've written a book featuring a doctor, a lawyer, or some other professional, it's important to give your manuscript to an expert for double-checking. I had a lawyer friend read my legal thriller, and he caught lots of legal mistakes I would have missed—and he saved me from being tarred and feathered by readers who've been to law school. When you use an expert as a test reader, be as generous with your thanks as they were with their time. Send them a check, a gift card, or the biggest gift basket you can find.

How many beta readers should you use? At least one, and a maximum of however many you can handle. I can find myself confused by too many opinions, and torn when opinions cancel each other out. But each writer is different, so offer your manuscript and see who steps up to read it.

If you're having trouble finding a good beta reader, go to your public library or look online for news about local writers' groups. Often these folks are willing to critique manuscripts or selected chapters, sometimes in a group meeting. Fellow writers can be the best—and the worst—beta readers. They can be harsh, since they are involved in the same effort, but they can also give great constructive feedback.

Your local bookstore might have an employee who loves to read and would be happy to be your test reader. Who knows? After your book is published, perhaps the manager will let you have an author signing in the store.

When your beta reader has finished reading, ask if they'd mind if you asked a few questions such as:

1) Was the protagonist likable? What did you like best about him or her? What did you like least?

2). Was the story credible? Did you have any problem believing the complications?

3). Did the ending seem contrived? Did the story wrap up too quickly or too slowly?

4.) How about the dialogue? Did it feel natural?

5.) Did the story drag at any point? Did it hold your interest through the middle?

6.) Was it an enjoyable read? Would you recommend it to your friends?

Once you've received feedback from your beta reader, make any changes needed in your manuscript. Listen again to any scenes you've edited. Once you're certain that all is as it should be, you're ready to create your submission draft, the draft you will send to a publisher.

THE SUBMISSION DRAFT

At some point you will have to release your book and send your baby to a publisher or agent.

Before you send it out, print your manuscript so that there are two manuscript pages per piece of paper, single space. (In other words, so it looks like a printed book.) Read this final draft as if it were a published novel. Or, if you have book formatting software like Vellum, go ahead and format the manuscript as if it were ready to be published, then print the pdf version.

Do not send it to a publisher or agent in this format —this is for your eyes only. It may sound crazy, but I see all kinds of mistakes when I'm reading a draft that looks like a book. Somehow my brain processes it differently, and my eyes pick up mistakes I have previously skimmed over.

After you've given the book a quick read and made any final adjustments, you're ready to send the manuscript.

If you want to traditionally publish, you will first send a proposal to an agent or editor (if the publisher even accepts unagented manuscripts). A proposal should contain a cover letter, a one-page synopsis, and the first three chapters of the novel.

In the query letter, include the back cover copy you wrote in the second draft (and have edited with each pass, right?). This should pique the editor's interest, the synopsis will prove you have a solid story structure, and the polished first three chapters will show the editor what sort of writer you are. The first chapter alone will tell him about your novel's genre, your protagonist, and your voice.

In the cover letter to the agent or editor, mention that the manuscript has been completed, and you'd love to send the entire thing. All you need is a green light . . .

If you want to self-publish, hire a professional editor to go through your manuscript. You don't want to hire someone to rewrite your novel; you want someone who will point out problems. Ask the editor to turn on "track changes" in Word so you can see where any changes were made and figure out *why* they were made. If you disagree with an editor's change, you can always reject the advice—but be sure you have a valid reason for dismissing it. I've found that my editors are nearly always right. (That's why they're editors).

After your book has been edited, you will need to have it formatted and you will need a professionally designed cover. You'll also need to purchase an ISBN number unless you plan to use Amazon's Kindle Direct Publishing program, which will give you a free ISBN.

Do I recommend KDP? Yes. I've published many books with them, including this one. It's easy, inexpensive (once you handle the editing and cover), and Amazon is the largest retailer in the world.

But Amazon is not the primary distributor for brick-and-mortar bookstores, so you may find it difficult, if not impossible, to find your book at a local bookshop . . . unless you know the owner.

Which road should you take? Unless you wrote your book for a specialty or niche market, you'll probably want to consider a traditional publisher first. If you can interest a traditional publisher, your book will receive professional editing, design, cover design, marketing, and sales support. You should also receive an advance against sales, a check you can enjoy any way you please (just don't forget to save some money for taxes. You won't see another check until you've sold enough books to actually earn that royalty).

The downside? You can expect to receive a royalty of anywhere from ten to twenty percent off the sales price—and in some instances, it may be the *net* sales price, which is usually the retail price minus forty or fifty percent.

I love speaking to children in schools, and I'm always tickled by their honest questions. I remember standing in front of one group of elementary kids. One little boy raised his hand, and when I nodded at him, he said, "So, are you like, *swimming* in money?"

I laughed. "No, I'm not." I then held up one of my picture books and told the kids that it sold in stores for about $14.99. "Of that fifteen dollars," I said, "how much do you think I get?"

"Six dollars?"

"Five?"

"Ten dollars!"

"Seven!"

You should have seen their crestfallen faces when I told them that I earned about twenty-five cents from the sale of each book. "Lots of people were involved in making this book," I explained. "The artist had to be paid. And the editor. And the designer. And the printer. And the salesmen. And the marketers. And the publicity person. And the truckers who hauled it to stores. And the bookstore who bought it to sell, and the clerk who sold it."

A writer who publishes with a traditional publisher has a great support team—but he or she has to pay them all, and we do it through lower royalties.

But something else comes with traditional publishing—credibility. When a book is traditionally published, almost everyone realizes that the book has hit a home run in the literary world, whether it's a best seller or not. That title has made it through vetting by an agent, an editor, a publisher, and a review committee. At least that many people considered it to be worthy of publishing, and that's no small matter.

Traditional publishing means your book has an opportunity to be carried in honest-to-goodness brick bookstores. They don't *have* to order your book, of course, but if the sales and marketing teams have done a good job, bookstores may order a copy or two. And replace them when those copies sell.

Perhaps the greatest advantage to traditional publishing is the fact that they pay you. I've had people ask me how much I had to pay to publish my books, and I was always surprised by the question, though not so much anymore. But for a writer who's trying to earn a living through publishing, that advance may be enough money to support the family a few months, and that's a godsend.

Getting a book published traditionally today isn't easy, but it may be the route you want to take. Unless your book is aimed for a specialty market, I would urge you to first try the traditional approach. Not only will it give you an appreciation for how the process works, but you may get some good editorial advice along the way.

Many publishers, however, will not look at your manuscript or proposal unless it comes from an agent . . . and finding a good agent can be as difficult as finding a publisher. Why? Because agents want to represent manuscripts they *know* they can sell. Few of them have time to spend on iffy projects.

Hundreds of books and articles have been written about how to get an agent, so I'm going to boil the advice down to the basics. First, do not sign with any agent who requires money from you up front. If they charge a reading or review fee, say thank you and walk away.

Second, remember that you are the employer and the agent is the employee, though the situation may feel quite the reverse. You may feel as though you are auditioning for Juilliard and lucky even to get an appointment, and truthfully, you may be. But you will be paying the agent if and when your manuscript sells, so do not allow yourself to be cowed. Neither, however, should you be bossy and demanding, as the author-agent relationship requires mutual respect in order to work.

The names of agents and agencies are easy to find on the Internet. As you read through those websites and listings, pay particular attention to the types of manuscripts each agent represents. If he or she doesn't handle children's books, don't send them a picture book manuscript. If they sell most of their titles to Harlequin and you don't write romance, perhaps this isn't the agent for you.

I sold seventeen books before I ever got an agent, but times have changed. Some smaller houses will consider unagented manuscripts, but most larger houses won't. Agents provide another layer of vetting or "winnowing out" for busy editors, and they appreciate the service agents provide.

If an agent tells you your manuscript isn't ready for publication, he or she is probably right. You can always get a second opinion, but you should also consider going back to the drawing board, checking your plot and character development, and doing another series of revisions. Do not decide to self-publish this manuscript.

If you self-publish a less-than-stellar manuscript, you may be shooting yourself in the foot. A slew of bad reviews on Amazon isn't going to help your future in publishing, and weak sales will hurt your prospects. Far better to consider that manuscript a learning experience and move on to another idea.

What if an agent or publisher tells you, "This is a good manuscript, but we simply can't find a place for it in our program?"

That's when you are free to consider another publisher who *can* find a place for it or consider self-publishing. If an agent or publisher tells you the manuscript is good, you have a green light for self-publishing (but you're going to miss out on the advantages of traditional publishing—namely, distribution, credibility, and higher sales numbers).

You should consider self-publishing if your book has received strong affirmation and:

--it's a title aimed at a niche market

--it has limited geographic appeal (i.e., a book about Florida law)

--it's an unusual format (like these writing lessons)

--it's so unique in design or format that no publisher knows what to do with it.

Publishers look for books that have the potential to sell thousands of copies—books that have wide appeal in a traditional, cost-effective format. If your book doesn't fit into that category, perhaps self-publishing is your answer.

Before giving up on the idea of traditional publishing, ask yourself:

- Have I honestly made this book the best it can be?

- Have I worked on it with a critique group or partner for honest feedback?
- Have I done the work—multiple drafts, careful self-editing, thorough research, attention to plot, theme, and characters?
- Have I sent it to a test reader or two (not family members) for honest feedback?
- Have I sent it to at least three carefully selected agents? Have any of them offered encouraging comments?
- Am I self-publishing only because I want to say I've published a book, or am I convinced this book has the best chance for success through self-publishing?

WHAT TO EXPECT NEXT

This section is geared toward those who opt for traditional publishing. If you choose self-publishing, the steps to publication can proceed at a quick pace. You will get your cover designed and your book formatted, then upload it to the sales platform of your choice. You could be holding your published book in a matter of days.

But if you opt for traditional publishing, be prepared to wait. If you send your work to an agent, you may wait months before you receive a reply. It's fine to send your query letter or email (a brief letter with a hook for your novel and a summary of your writing experience) to several agents at once, just be polite enough to mention that you're making a simultaneous submission. Ask if you may send the complete manuscript or a proposal with the first three chapters.

If you receive a positive reply, send a cover letter, the synopsis, and the first three chapters and be prepared to wait again. If several agents want to see your proposal, that's fine —in fact, it may light a fire under someone and nudge them to reply sooner. But let the agent know that you are simultaneously submitting.

Once you sign with an agent, however, you can no longer flirt with other agents. The contract you sign with an agency will declare that he or she will represent all your literary works until one or both of the parties desires to terminate the relationship.

When and if your agent sells your book, you will be offered a contract for publishing rights. You will probably also be asked for audio rights, foreign rights, ebook rights, and other miscellaneous rights. Your agent will help you negotiate for these (or not), and then you will sign the contract.

One note: When you receive your advance and any future royalty payments, a designated percentage will go to your agent (the standard at this time is 15 percent). Even if you fire your agent, that split will continue as long as that book is being printed under the terms of that contract. Your agent will receive his or her commission as long as the book is in print—after all, they earned it.

I've found that a lot of writers are confused when they hear about "rights." There are publishing rights and copyrights. When you create a work, whether its a book, a poem, a piece of music, or a photograph, under U.S. law you own the copyright whether or not you register it with the copyright office. When you sign a book contract, you are not selling the copyright—you're selling the right to publish your book in (the world, English-speaking countries, OR the U.S.) in certain formats. Be sure to read your contract carefully so you know which rights you're selling. You can always strike through certain clauses (if, for instance, you don't want to sell dramatic rights because you want to publish it as a play), but most publishers want to buy all rights. This is why you need an agent to help you negotiate.

After the contract is signed, signing, your agent will ask for the entire manuscript, and he or she will begin to send your proposal to publishers. Again, you'll wait. An editor will read it—if they pass, your agent will get an email saying so. If the editor likes what she sees, she will ask for the entire manuscript, so it's a good thing you have it ready to go, right?

Once the editor reads the entire manuscript, if he likes the novel, he may have other editors read it, too. If they like it as well, it will go before an editorial committee meeting, where other company employees will discuss the book and whether or not the company can successfully sell it. The marketing people will have a strong voice. Those in the marketing department may suggest a new title or offer ideas about the cover.

If the publishing committee agrees to buy the rights to publish your book, you will receive a contract, which you will discuss with your agent. Your agent will negotiate to get the best deal possible for you in terms of marketing, advance, number of author copies, and publication date (usually about a year after the contract is signed). Go ahead and celebrate, but your work is not yet finished.

When a traditional publisher publishes your book, they will register the copyright. If you self-publish, you can register the copyright yourself or not—it's completely up to you. For information about registering a copyright yourself, visit https://www.copyright.gov/registration/.

Once your editor has the complete manuscript, she will read it with an editorial eye and then you'll receive a letter filled with suggested changes. This is called the "substantive" or "macro" edit.

Don't be offended—your editor is the expert, remember? Don't fight over molehills, but do stand up for your beliefs if an editor challenges something you feel is truly important. You will revise your manuscript yet again, making the suggested editorial changes, and submit it again. Label that file "BookTitle FINAL draft" and save it on your computer.

Then the substantive editor will pass your manuscript

along to a line editor, who will go through your book line by line, checking punctuation, spelling, and readability. If you're fortunate, they'll do it with "track changes" on, so you'll be able to see—and learn from—the changes made.

After that, the manuscript will go to a copy editor, and then to a proofreader. Each publishing house is different, but you will receive a copy of your book at various times in this process. You will be able to review the changes made, or maybe something will occur to you and you'll change your original copy. Just remember—the farther along in the process, the less tinkering you will be able to do. Once the book is typeset and every word positioned on the page, you can't make huge changes. Doing so, even if allowed, could throw off the publishing schedule and delay your book's release.

Finally you will receive copies of the printed pages—this is called a *galley*. I used to receive these on sheets of paper; these days I often receive electronic versions. Your publisher will have its own way of doing things.

And then the book goes to press. Your previously-messy baby will have been edited several times, designed, proofread, measured, printed, digitized, and possibly even recorded as an audio book.

Then it will graduate from finishing school and enter the world. I've published dozens of books, but I still thrill to open a package and hold my polished "baby" in my hands.

Is all the work worth it?

You bet.

THE FINAL DRAFT

Your book is published . . . so why did I tell you to save a file of your final draft?

Because most books do not remain in print forever.

If, one day, your book goes out of print and *if* your contract has a rights reversion clause that covers all editions, the publishing rights will revert to you.

Sometimes—even without a rights reversion clause in your contract—a publisher will revert rights to you if sales have slowed to a trickle and you ask for a rights reversion. Sometimes they won't.

But if they do, you'll be glad you had that final file. You'll need a new cover, of course, and a new ISBN number for your new edition. Then you'll be free to self-publish your book and enthrall a new generation of readers.

RESOURCES

Books:
The Breakout Novelist, by Donald Maass. Any book by Donald Maass, actually.
Stein on Writing, by Sol Stein.
How to Grow a Novel, by Sol Stein.
Self-Editing for Fiction Writers, by Renni Browne and Dave King.

Websites:
Writer Beware: a site to protect writers from unscrupulous agents, agencies, publishers, etc.
http://www.sfwa.org/other-resources/for-authors/writer-beware/
AAR: Association of Author's Representatives, a list of agents who have agreed to uphold a standard of ethics
http://aaronline.org

Self-publishing:
http://bookbaby.com
http://smashwords.com

http://kdp.amazon.com
http://www.kobo.com
http://nookpress.com
https://play.google.com/books/publish/

Vellum, an easy-to-use tool to format your book:
https://vellum.pub/

Scrivener, the best program I've found for writing your book —with a generous free trial: http://literatureandlatte.com

Audio Book Production for self-published titles:
http://www.acx.com

Marketing:

http://bookmarketingtools.com

For $29.00, at this site you can submit your free or low-cost ebook to dozens of sites and newsletters.

http://bookbub.com

It's not easy to get a slot or ad on Bookbub, but it's worth it.

U.S. Copyright Office:

When a traditional publisher publishes your book, they will register the copyright. If you self-publish, you can register the copyright yourself or not—it's completely up to you. For information about registering a copyright, visit https://www.copyright.gov/registration/.

THANK YOU!

Thank you for purchasing this lesson in **Writing Lessons from the Front.** If you find any typos in this book, please write and let us know where they are: hunthaven@gmail.com.

We would also appreciate it if you would be kind enough to leave a review of this book on Amazon. Thank you!

ABOUT THE AUTHOR

With nearly six million copies of her books sold worldwide, Angela Hunt is the best-selling author of more than 165 works ranging from picture books (*The Tale of Three Trees*) to novels and nonfiction.

Now that her two children are grown, Angie and her husband live in Florida with Very Big Dogs (a direct result of watching *Turner and Hooch* too many times) and assorted chickens. Her affinity for mastiffs has not been without its rewards—one of their dogs was featured on *Live with Regis and Kelly* as the second-largest canine in America. Their dog received this dubious honor after an all-expenses-paid trip to Manhattan for the dog and the Hunts, complete with VIP air travel and a stretch limo in which they toured New York City. Afterward, the dog gave out pawtographs at the airport.

Her books have won the coveted Christy Award, several Angel Awards from Excellence in Media, and the Gold and Silver Medallions from *Foreword Magazine*'s Book of the Year Award. In 2007, her novel *The Note* was featured as a Christmas movie on the Hallmark channel. She has completed a doctorate in biblical literature and another in Theology.

When she's not home writing, Angie often travels to teach writing workshops at schools and writers' conferences. And to talk about her animals, of course. Readers may visit her web site at www.angelahuntbooks.com.

Made in the USA
Columbia, SC
02 July 2023